POWERFUL AFFIRMATIONS FOR FEMPRENEURS

VOLUME 2

A Success Tool for Kingdom
Business Women

Visionary Author
Nadia Francois

Powerful Affirmations for FemPreneurs
Volume 2
Copyright © 2023
by Heiress International Enterprises

All rights reserved. No part of this book may be reproduced or transmitted in any form or by any means without written permission from the author.

Printed in the USA

DEDICATION

This book is dedicated to kingdom women in business that believe in the power of affirming themselves and praying over their businesses constantly. God's promises for our lives are right on the other side of faith. Each of our journey is different as we encounter ups and downs along the way but we must keep the faith and stay positive through it all. The prayers, affirmations and letters of encouragement in this book are words of inspiration from one business woman to another.

AUTHOR DIRECTORY

Angela Thomas Smith - Foreword	3
Nadia Francois – Visionary	10
Vashiti Bratton	16
Celeste Payne	23
Brenda B. Myers	30
Dr. Valerie Richardson	37
Monique S. Robinson	43
Dr. Shirley Boykins Bryant	50
Angelica Carmouche	58
Vanessa J. Ross	65
Brenda Sawyer	72
Dr. Josephine Harris	79
Dr. Sandy Sanders	85
Dr. Feleshia Borskey Young	95

FOREWORD

The Importance of Affirmations

As a Woman Entrepreneur, it's very important for us to have strategies in place to keep us from getting complacent. Understanding the P.O.W.E.R that we possess within us, in Proverbs 18:20-21 (NIV) it says 20 From the fruit of their mouth a person's stomach is filled; with the harvest of their lips, they are satisfied. 21 The tongue has the power of life and death, and those who love it will eat its fruit."Know that God has Positioned us to be Overcomers by being a Willing vessel to be used for his glory to Educate, Empower and Encourage others to lead by example because of our Resilience. The word of GOD clearly tells us we have the P.O.W.E.R, to ! What will you speak over your life and why?

The Importance of Putting into Daily Practice (PDP)

It has been proving that if you practice something over a certain period it will become a habit. Philippa Lally, PhD, a senior researcher at University College London, PhD found in a study it takes about 66 days— more than two months – to form a habit. Speaking daily Affirmations over our lives is a great habit to have, replacing those negative thoughts with positive thoughts will allow you to change your mindset and outlook on life. If you want to see your business go to the next level, I dare you to take to the knowledge and wisdom shared in this book and apply it to your life.

The Importance of Covering our Business

Prayer still works, acknowledging God and understanding that all things are possible through him. We are powerless without him but, when you allow God's covering the spiritual protection and nurture which only God provides for all those who are in a covenant relationship with him through prayer. So always remember to put God first by praying and giving thanks.

Allow yourself to Reset, Renew and Release as you take this journey with these Women Entrepreneur sharing things that worked for them. Take a moment to reflect on your why for starting your business and as you flip through these pages. Remember the P.O.W.E.R within.

BY AUTHOR ANGELA THOMAS SMITH

ANGELA THOMAS SMITH

Angela is the youngest of 4 and both parents have gone on to glory. She's an author of over 50 books, she hosts 4 podcast shows and she is the proud owner of Aspiring Authors Magazine. Angela has a passion for people and the word of God. Angela has been featured on several News stations, radios and newspapers. Angela believes in what she calls the E3Experience and everyone she encounters she wants them to leave EDUCATED, EMPOWERED AND ENCOURAGED to stay in the race and not give up!!!!

I can do all things through Christ who strengthens me.

Philippians 4:13 NKJV

DAILY AFFIRMATIONS

The Evolution of the FemPreneur

DAY ONE

Everyday is a NEW day. Another chance to get it right.

DAY TWO

I will prioritize self-care daily. Mental and physical wellness are my portion.

DAY THREE

If God led me to it, He will guide me through it. I can have the desires of my heart.

DAY FOUR

I will work smart and not hard in achieving my goals.

DAY FIVE

I will maintain a positive mindset no matter what comes my way.

DAY SIX

I am confident, fierce and courageous. Ready for my divine assignment.

DAY SEVEN

I celebrate myself for achieving major and minor accomplishments. Every step matters.

BY AUTHOR NADIA FRANCOIS

PRAYER

Father God, Thank you. Thank you for the opportunity to serve your people and to fulfill my purpose as a woman owned business in the marketplace. Father God as I embark on this journey trusting your promises for my life, please give me the guidance, discernment, and grace to complete the assignment. Lord, I thank you for your grace and mercy, your unconditional love and acceptance. I thank you for peace that surpasses all understanding Father. Lord I ask that you open my mind to accept all the things that you have in store for my life. Help me to align my business and my personal obligations where I can be the mother, wife, sister, friend and entrepreneur that you called me to be, Lord. And Lord please help me to be a good steward over all the blessings that you will provide through my business and hard work. Help me to help others and to keep a servant's heart. Help me to maintain my mental and physical health so that I can execute as my best self. Thank you for divine connections, innovative ideas, and the will to win. Lord I thank you in advance for these and all your blessings. In Jesus' name, Amen.

BY AUTHOR NADIA FRANCOIS

LETTER OF ENCOURAGEMENT

Dear FemPreneur,

I want you to know that this isn't an easy road but it is a conquerable one. Owning, running, and maintaining a business is hard work and not for the faint at heart. Becoming a successful business owner means that you can't run with the crowd, you may miss out on some things, and you have to be diligent in your journey but it is well worth the sacrifice. Here are 3 success strategies that I have used along my journey as an entrepreneur that I hope can help you along your journey:

1. **Maintain a positive mindset.**

No matter what comes our way, we must remain positive and optimistic. Entrepreneurship is risky and keeping this in mind will help through the low points and propel you in the high points.

2. **Don't do business in your feelings.**

When we bring our feelings into our business decisions bad judgement can occur. We never want to act off of feelings rather off of facts. We are in business to make money so the best decisions are informed and profitable.

3. Don't despise small beginnings.

There are levels in business and what one business requires may not necessarily be what is required in another.

Organize your business needs and prioritize your business growth according to where you are.

Your business is your baby. Nurture it and raise it up to support itself. Be Bold, Be Courageous, and Be Consistent. You've Got This!!

NADIA FRANCOIS

Nadia Francois is a serial entrepreneur with a heart for people. A hairstylist by trade, Nadia holds current licenses in Cosmetology and Barbering, a B.S. in Business Administration and a certificate in Women's Entrepreneurship. The Louisiana native began her entrepreneurial journey at the age of 19 and has used her experiences and knowledge to help other business owners start and grow their ventures. In 2019, she was nominated for Business Woman of the Year by the Greater Southwest Louisiana Black Chamber of Commerce. July 2020, the What's Your Super Power Empire began with an anthology and expanded into the digital tv world. In 2021, Nadia continued to enhance her digital footprint with the addition of Power Conversations Magazine & Podcast which are additional extensions of her WYSP Digital Media which caters to minority entrepreneurs and their advancement. In 2022, Nadia was awarded the "Game Changer" award by the Beauty Industry Community Awards Organization, has spoken on various global platforms and is launching her newest #1 Best-Selling Book, A Mother's Prayer Anthology.

Connect with Nadia at www.nadiafrancois.com

He who is faithful in what is least is faithful also in much; and he who is unjust in what is least is unjust also in much.

Luke 16:10 NKJV

DAILY AFFIRMATIONS

Every Day Is A New Day, Loaded with New Benefits

DAY ONE

My gift of today will be fully enjoyed.

DAY TWO

Today I walk into an Amazing day where Amazing things happen.

DAY THREE

Today I will began to live the life I am destined to and grateful for.

DAY FOUR

Greatness, Goodness, and Mercy is following me all the days of my life.

DAY FIVE

I walk in favor wherever I go and with whomever I meet.

DAY SIX

I am Healthy, Wealthy, and Wise.

DAY SEVEN

I am the epitome of Grace, Confidence, & Kindness.

BY AUTHOR VASHITI BRATTON

PRAYER

God, thank you for this day, the one that you have made, let us rejoice and be glad in it. Thanking you that it's never too late to start over, get back up again, or even start a new thing. You are God and besides you there is no other. You are the teacher of all teachers, the leader of all leaders, thank you for your divine instructions for leading us and guiding us and showing us the right way to go. For making all of the crooked places straight and the high places low. For bringing us before great men and causing our name to become great. We thank you for every breakthrough, for every turn around, every new opportunity, every new ideal, to you be the glory for crowning our heads with wisdom, knowledge, and most of all understanding for allowing to walk in the path you have set before us, not looking to the left nor the right but keeping our fixed on you and trusting you with all of our hearts that you will direct us in the right directions. To you be the glory we submit ourselves and our businesses into your very capable hands, have thy own way and be ye glorified in every area of our lives and every part of our day. In Jesus name we pray, Amen.

BY AUTHOR VASHITI BRATTON

LETTER OF ENCOURAGEMENT

Dear Sis,

Forgetting those things that are behind us and pressing toward the mark of a higher calling, 'Let's go Sis.' Don't be afraid of new beginnings, don't be afraid to start over, don't be afraid to add on/to or launch out. Every day is a new day, a new opportunity to be the best version of who you are and what you are destined to be. There are so many times I have thought about quitting, but God comes along and says NO, there is still so much more. Get up, dust yourself off, take all the lessons you have learned and move forward, stay on the path, stay focused, and watch things change for you and your business. Every day we open our eyes is a gift, take that gift and appreciate it to the fullest, use it to the best of your ability, enjoy all the benefits of that gift, and allow your business to flourish day by day. It is with great anticipation that our days ahead will be amazing and what's to come will be greater than what has been. God has great things in store just for you, take your place Sis, your time is TODAY.

BY AUTHOR VASHITI BRATTON

VASHITI BRATTON

Elder Vashiti Bratton is first and foremost anointed by God. She is an honorable woman of God, dynamic preacher/teacher of the precious Word of God, and a mentor to many. Elder Bratton currently serves as First Assistant at Antioch Full Gospel Baptist Church under the leadership of her Pastor Bishop Gregory Cooper, Sr. in Baton Rouge, LA. In 1997, Elder Bratton accepted her call into ministry under the leadership of Bishop Gregory Cooper, Sr. whom she very highly esteems in the Lord along with Elder Bessie Cooper. More than 35 years ago under the tutelage of the late Pastor Edith Howard, she gladly accredits her with being saved, sanctified, and filled with the Holy Ghost, walking in holiness, and instilling in her a firm foundation.

Her educational accomplishments include a bachelor's degree in bible and theology from Faith Christian University. She obtained an associate degree and certification from the Paralegal Institute of Louisiana State University. She holds credentials as an ordained elder from The College of Ordained Elders of the Full Gospel Baptist Church Fellowship International. She is also a certified belief counselor with a concentration on marriage and family. Elder Bratton is married to a wonderful husband, Deacon Frederick Bratton and together they are the proud parents of 8 children and are blessed to enjoy 13 of their grandest blessings which is their grandchildren.

Above all, Elder Bratton is adamant about empowering God's people to live a victorious life of holiness by rightly dividing the word of God in such a way that it will impact and bring health, healing, and deliverance to its listeners. Elder Bratton leads a life of holiness by walking in love and extending that love to all she encounters. She believes that the word of God is truth and can set us free from any form of bondage. While in turn causing God's people to live holy and acceptable unto God without compromise.

I will remain confident. #lovecovers

Commit your works to the Lord, And your thoughts will be established.

Proverbs 16:3 NKJV

DAILY AFFIRMATIONS

I Love Me Some Me Fempreneur Style

DAY ONE

I not only respect and admire others, I respect and admire myself.

DAY TWO

I am valuable to God, my family, my community, and the world, and I treat myself as though I am.

DAY THREE

I am a miracle that was carefully and intentionally created to be an answer in the Earth.

DAY FOUR

I am not a mistake or a disappointment rather, a masterpiece with great purpose and a great future.

DAY FIVE

I confront and replace all negative self talk, which is idle and foolish talk, with positive declarations and decrees which build pathways to my success and well being.

DAY SIX

I quickly identify and shift my position/placement in business or personal relationships that cause damage, injury or loss to me physically, mentally, emotionally or financially.

DAY SEVEN

I am a rocket booster who affirms other women to push them forward and refuse to take the bait of a blocker and hold another sister down.

BY AUTHOR CELESTE PAYNE

PRAYER

Father in the name of Jesus, I pray for every fempreneur. Holy Spirit speak to each fempreneurs heart and let them know that you always, at all times are available and accessible for counsel and advisement. Holy Spirit, take your part in their lives. Lead, guide, sanctify a clear path for your business leaders. Illuminate the right relationships and contracts. Remind them of what they have learned in the past and show them things to come. Help them properly appropriate their time between business, family and personal care. I pray for health, wealth and a fruitful and meaningful life to all in Jesus Name. Amen

BY AUTHOR CELESTE PAYNE

LETTER OF ENCOURAGEMENT

Dear Fempreneur,

I want you to know that God is with you every step of the way. God is our refuge and strength [mighty and impenetrable]. He is always ready, present, and well-proven to help in times of trouble. So we will not fear when the earth changes, when earthquakes come and the mountains crumble into the sea. God dwells within her [His city]; she will not be moved, nor can she be destroyed. From the very break of day, God will protect her. (Psalm 46:1-5 NIV, AMP, NLT) You are God's city, equipped with the creativity needed to solve problems and overcome obstacles. You were established to prosper. Don't be discouraged or give up hope. Keep moving forward. God is with you every step of the way. You will not fail. With God all things are possible to her that believes. Keep believing in you Sis. Keep believing in God. Keep believing that God is working through you.

Sincerely, Celeste Payne

BY AUTHOR CELESTE PAYNE

CELESTE PAYNE

In a world where chaos and conflict abounds, it's essential to infuse creativity in all that we do as an escape from the tension and confusion that we may experience. Celeste Payne is a best-selling author, artist and educator and owner of Chortazo Fine Art Gallery. She combines art with self-care strategies to help her clients relax, de-stress, and discover innovative solutions to barriers that may be hindering their success. Through courses, books, virtual and in- person paint parties, and empowerment workshops her clients can Advance, Resurge, and Thrive using the arts as a highway to life transformation.

www.chortazoarts.com

@chortazoarts

But remember the Lord your God, for it is he who gives you the ability to produce wealth, and so confirms his covenant, which he swore to your ancestors, as it is today.

Deuteronomy 8:18 NKJV

DAILY AFFIRMATIONS

7 Daily Affirmations for Self-Love, Confidence and Manifesting

DAY ONE

I am BOLD and I will walk in my boldness unapologetically.

DAY TWO

It is not my timing but God's timing and I know what He has for me is for me.

DAY THREE

I am strong, I am powerful, I am magnificent and my light shines wherever I go.

DAY FOUR

Doors are opening, walls are going down and I have a seat at the table.

DAY FIVE

I focus only on the things that I can change, and I give no power to the things that I cannot change.

DAY SIX

My greater is already here.

DAY SEVEN

My business and my life get better every day. I will receive all the desires of my heart.

BY AUTHOR BRENDA B. MYERS

PRAYER

Most gracious and mighty God, I come to you as humbly as I know how. Thanking you for who you are. Dear Heavenly Father I pray that you continue to be a shield around each of us as we continue on our journey through life. I pray that the coming years are the best years yet. Bless our businesses, oh Lord. Protect our families and friends. Help us to make sound decision and that we allow you to be the head all that we do, for we know that with you all things are possible. In Jesus Name, Amen

BY AUTHOR BRENDA B. MYERS

LETTER OF ENCOURAGEMENT

My Dearest Fempreneur,

Keep going! Even though the road may seem rough at times, you must always remember that you won't get to where you want to go if you give up. The lessons are in the failures. They teach us what not to do next time. They will lead you to the pathway of your purpose. Also, remember that your opinion of you is the only one that matters. And as you walk through life with confidence, believing in who you are, others will see your shining light. It will shine so bright that it will precede you when you enter a room. I was always told that if you are going to be in the room, be in the room. What do I mean by that? Well, if you were in a meeting, or at a party and no one remembers that you were there, then you were not "in the room." You should resonate so much light that people are drawn to you. Let your light speak for itself. One of the most important lessons in life is to not let others project their idea of you onto you. You should be who you are called to be.

God created you the way you are and only He can change you. Often in business, people tend to give their opinion of what you should be doing. What does that mean? It means that if you share your idea, dream or vision with someone who never had an idea, dream or vision, they might not see things the same as you. For instance, if you tell your friend that you are thinking about opening a nail salon, but your friend tells you that you are good at doing hair and that she thinks you should open a hair salon instead, don't let that discourage you from your path. That is only their opinion. You continue to stay steadfast on your beliefs and your goals.

The key takeaways are to always be true to yourself, never take anything for granted, trust God and put Him ahead of everything you do and always believe in yourself. Life is a marathon, not a sprint.

Love,
Brenda B. Myers
Entrepreneur, Author, Speaker, Mentor

BY AUTHOR BRENDA B. MYERS

BRENDA B. MYERS

Brenda Myers is an entrepreneur, author, public speaker and mentor. She is the Owner of Journey Insurance Solutions, LLC, which is certified by the Mississippi Minority Business Enterprise as a minority and woman-owned business. Mrs. Myers is also a Financial Broker licensed to do business in Mississippi, Tennessee, Louisiana and Texas. She is the President/Founder of Entrepreneurs Academy 101, which is an online program to teach aspiring or beginner entrepreneurs how to start and grow their own business. She is the Founder/Chairman of Entrepreneurs Academy 101

Foundation, which is a nonprofit organization created to provide scholarships and training for high school students who want to pursue entrepreneurship. Mrs. Myers is the author of three books, "Becoming an Entrepreneur – Learn How to Start and Grow Your Business," "The Productive Entrepreneur – the secret to getting everything done," and "Making the Decision to Purchase Life Insurance." She is a member of Women for Progress of MS, Inc., an organization that promotes cultural advancement and economic development while empowering women through Women's Business & Entrepreneur's Network. She's a member of NAIFA (National Association of Insurance and Financial Advisors), and a member of Power to Exhale Central Mississippi Chapter, which is an organization that promotes female empowerment and community service. She has spoken at several summits, conferences and virtual events. Her studies include Jackson State University and Tulane University where she pursued her degree in Public Relations. Mrs. Myers was named one of the Top 50 Women Empowering Women in 2022 and Who's Who in America 2021- 2022. She has been featured on several media platforms such as Stilettos on the Pavement, Defining Moments, and Metro Mornings Live. She has also been featured in New York Weekly publication, Woman to Woman the magazine, and Our Mississippi magazine. Above all, her greatest accomplishment is being the proud parent of twins, a boy and a girl, and grandmother to four amazing grandchildren.

Then the Lord answered me and said: "Write the vision And make it plain on tablets, That he may run who reads it.

Habakkuk 2:2 NKJV

DAILY AFFIRMATIONS

Purpose-Driven Affirmations

DAY ONE
Everything is in my life is coming into alignment and working together for my good

DAY TWO
I am overwhelmed with the strength, peace, joy, and wisdom of God

DAY THREE
My days are exhausted with purpose and God's will for my life is manifesting daily

DAY FOUR
I am royalty; therefore, I expect and receive royal treatment in every area of my life.

DAY FIVE
I am worthy of good things, and I will have good success.

DAY SIX
My life is a testament of the goodness, grace, glory, and favor of God.

DAY SEVEN

I am prospering and in good health even as my soul is prospering.

BY AUTHOR DR. VALERIE RICHARDSON

PRAYER

Lord, I pray that you would remind my sister that she was created on purpose for purpose and destined for greatness. Remind her that she is wonderfully made just as she is. Remind her that her life and experiences were uniquely designed by you to complete her assignment. Deliver her from any deceptive spirits of comparison and competition. Remind your daughter that she is the apple of your eye, more precious than rubies, royal and an heir unto your kingdom. Give her the strength, power, provisions, people, and faith to manifest the vision that you've given her. Remind her that your love and promises are unconditional. I come against any negative thoughts, people, things, and ungodly assignments that try to hinder her progress, promotion, and productivity. Lord, whatever she sets her hand to do, bless it. I speak abundance, purpose, grace, mercy, peace, and victory over my sister. In Jesus Name. Amen

BY AUTHOR DR. VALERIE RICHARDSON

LETTER OF ENCOURAGEMENT

Hey Sis,

Just know that you are not in this alone and I got you so don't give up! I want you to know that I believe in you, and I got you. My desire is that you succeed in every area of your life, so Sis, I got you! Please understand that I'm your coopetition not your competition. So, if you need help executing your vision, I got you. If you need my support, I got you! If you need me to hold your hand, I got you. If you need me to encourage or pray with you, I got you.

Always remember that you can do all things through Christ and giving up is not an option! No matter what you go through, remember that God is working all things together for your good and if you stay connected, confident, committed and consistent, it shall come to pass! Love you!

BY AUTHOR DR. VALERIE RICHARDSON

DR. VALERIE RICHARDSON

Dr. Valerie Richardson has many years of experience as a Registered Dietitian, researcher, educator, clinician, and consultant. She is a business owner, licensed funeral director and life insurance agent.

She is also the author of "The Vision Blueprint." Valerie is a servant and ministry leader who finds joy in accommodating the needs of others through community service efforts that equip and elevate minority women and girls. This desire prompted the birth of her business, "She Whealthy, Inc. which focuses on nurturing and equipping minority women with vital knowledge, tools and resources that promote wholeness, advancement and success.

Connect with her at: www.drvalerierich.com

For as he thinks in his heart, so is he.

Proverbs 23:7 NKJV

DAILY AFFIRMATIONS

Leaving Behind Failure and Doubt to be Successful

DAY ONE

You can do exceedingly and abundantly above all you ask or think.

DAY TWO

I create my own destiny and outcomes.

DAY THREE

I Know I am Enough.

DAY FOUR

Being Me is How I WIN.

DAY FIVE

I Trust the Timing of My Life.

DAY SIX

My Actions Match My Goals.

DAY SEVEN

Shine to Help Everyone Shine Around You.

BY AUTHOR MONIQUE S. ROBINSON

PRAYER

Dear God, I pray the women reading this will be touched by the words that you have given me to use to minister to them as we are growing our businesses, skills, and revenue. I pray that you will allow us to decrease so the work of the kingdom can be done. Thank you, Lord, for providing us the gifts to be used as vessels for your work. Amen

BY AUTHOR MONIQUE S. ROBINSON

LETTER OF ENCOURAGEMENT

Dear Future Millionaire,

Hello, I hope this letter finds you well. I know that the daily work of being successful can be challenging but you are capable of all the demands and opportunities coming your way. Sometimes the world seems to be challenging in the daily hustle just breath, step back and make it happen. Also, don't be afraid of failure, making mistakes, and testing yourself. Please know that nothing Beats Failure but a Try. So, there is a big world made for your successful journey so Make it Happen.

Your Sis, Monique Robinson

BY AUTHOR MONIQUE S. ROBINSON

MONIQUE S. ROBINSON

Monique S. Robinson received a B.A from Wilberforce University; Psychology, M. Ed from Concordia University-Portland; Educational Leadership, and Ed. S from Northcentral University; Educational Leadership.

M. Robinson is the founder of A Better Chance for Youth Futures Inc. a nonprofit organization that promotes higher learning for all scholars. Advocates for Historically Black Colleges and Universities. While providing consulting services on grant writing, scholar preparation letters, and test preparation. In addition, in 2009 received the Teacher of the Year award for Imagine Schools, district, and region for her contributions to education.

Do you see a man who excels in his work? He will stand before kings; He will not stand before unknown men.

Proverbs 22:29 NKJV

DAILY AFFIRMATIONS

I Am the Woman for the Assignment

DAY ONE
As I rise daily, I stand in the favor and walk in the purpose that GOD has set forth for me before the beginning of time.

DAY TWO
I am intelligent and everything I put my hands to do shall be a success.

DAY THREE
My business and my purpose are one and the same.

DAY FOUR
I am worthy of success in my home and in my business.

DAY FIVE
GOD has good plans for me and my business. Plans not of harm, but of a good end.

DAY SIX
My business has been ordained by the kingdom of GOD; therefore, it shall be prosperous.

DAY SEVEN

I stand in alignment with positive energy and great abundance.

BY AUTHOR DR. SHIRLEY BOYKINS BRYANT

PRAYER

Father GOD, Jesus, Holy Spirit I start this day by thanking you for your presence in my life and in my business. I invite your presence and discernment in every word that I speak, every person that I speak to and every decision that I make concerning the life of my family and my business. I ask that you be a shield of protection from persons or energy that might enter into my path and are not a part of your ordained purpose for this day. I ask that you anoint me with the strength needed to do the things I need to do, to make this day a success and ensure that it is aligned with your will and purpose for my business, and my life. I ask for the discipline needed to stay the course in those times when life and business are challenging. I ask that you continue to lead and guide me through this journey, and I will continue to give you all the Praise, Honor and Glory in the Mighty Name of Jesus, I Pray – AMEN!

BY AUTHOR DR. SHIRLEY BOYKINS BRYANT

LETTER OF ENCOURAGEMENT

Dear Sister!

When times are challenging in business and in life, as we know that they sometimes will be. Take the necessary time to breathe, refocus, rejuvenate, and restart. Tell yourself that I can do this because I am the woman for this assignment. My father, who is the creator of this universe, has my back. He ordained me for this purpose, therefore there is nothing I cannot do. Know that GOD is faithful and is ensuring that your name is being mentioned in rooms your feet have yet to enter. Every door that GOD opens for you, you will shine as you walk through it. Spend time wisely, with those who see your value. You may not be their first choice, but you are GODs chosen one. Give yourself some grace and be heavy on self-forgiveness. We all have stumbled, yet we persisted. Quitting can never be an option. Surround yourself with those who fiercely love, not tolerate you. Connect with those who share your energy, Its perfectly okay to prioritize your mental and physical self-care.

Your future shines as bright as the optimism in your laugh, the positive energy you exude and the love that you give others. This Is the Year, that you will get unstuck in habits that do not serve you in life and in business. You will penetrate the emotional blocks, find real clarity, and implement the habits that you need to evolve in the next greatest season of your life and business. May the Peace of GOD continue to lead and guide you daily.

BY AUTHOR DR. SHIRLEY BOYKINS BRYANT

DR. SHIRLEY BOYKINS BRYANT

Dr. Shirley Boykins Bryant hails from the great state of Texas. She is an Author, Youth Behavioral Coach and Chief Operating Officer of Let's Talk About It - Behavioral Coaching LLC and Educating Our Youth, which is a non-profit organization. She is employed as a Human Resources Policy Manager for a federal government organization and Adjunct Professor for Bay Atlantic University, Washington D.C. Shirley has a Doctorate Degree in Human and Organizational Psychology; she is a certified Emotional Intelligence and Cognitive Behavior Practitioner and has a Diploma in Modern Applied

Psychology. She has written and published research titled "The Lived Experiences of Federal Human Resources Professionals during the COVID-19 Pandemic" and Co-Authored several Amazon International Best Seller Anthologies.

Unless the Lord builds the house, the builders labor in vain. Unless the Lord watches over the city, the guards stand watch in vain.

Psalms 127:1 NKJV

DAILY AFFIRMATIONS

Affirmations for a Strong Mind

DAY ONE

I am strong because the Lord is my strength when I feel weak.

DAY TWO

I am courageous because the Lord has not given me a spirit of fear but one of sound mind, perfect clarity and perfect peace.

DAY THREE

My family, my belongings and I are protected because the Lord is our refuge and causes no harm to come near our tent.

DAY FOUR

My health is protected because although a thousand may fall at my side, ten thousand at my right hand, it will not come near me.

DAY FIVE

I am victorious because God fights my battles.

DAY SIX

I am clothed with strength and dignity I am covered by his grace and mercy.

DAY SEVEN

I am loved beyond measure; I am the apple of my Father God's eye; I am His treasure.

BY AUTHOR ANGELICA CARMOUCHE

PRAYER

Father, I come to you with praises lifted, and heart ready to receive all the goodness and light you have for me. I thank you Lord God for all you have done to bless me and my family asking that you continue to surround us with the white protective light of your Holy Spirit as we walk in deeper fellowship with Him, the Holy Spirit of our Lord God Jesus Christ. Lord, please bless us with your wisdom, and Grace and Mercy. Bless us with the peace that surpasses all understanding as we experience what it means to truly lean into your word. In Jesus name we pray. Amen

BY AUTHOR ANGELICA CARMOUCHE

LETTER OF ENCOURAGEMENT

Dear FemPreneur,

I know the struggle can be real when you are starting a new business or have been working a business for a while; you may start to feel like there is no movement towards your dreams, emotions can get a hold of you and/or life happens. You may feel weighed down, distracted, depressed, overwhelmed, stuck in a rut; unable to act or even know what the next step towards action is. You may even have had a plan of action mapped out in your mind, but it is not hitting like you thought it would. I want to let you know before you sit down and think about giving up bring your plans to God in prayer and have faith. Recognizing the seasons of Prayer/Faith, Prepare, Shift, Serve and Move will help you along your way.

As we pray in faith God is working on our behalf, you may not see it all yet, but prayer doors are being opened as you knock in faith. I truly believe that Prayer and Faith open doors.

If you are praying in faith and you feel like nothing is happening understand that this is time of wait. In this time don't do nothing! Prepare! Create! Make! A waiting season is not a season to waste it is the time to hone your skills. Preparation equals elevation. If you are feeling stuck, overwhelmed with emotion or depressed the only way to break those chains is to Pray, Shift, Move and Serve. Pray and shift your focus off yourself and onto someone else. The best way to do this is to serve.

Get up and move even if it is serving in your own household, your family, your children, your spouse or in church. Feed someone who cannot afford a meal, give a gift to a cancer patient, sing in the choir at church, serve out in the community. Shifting the focus onto something or someone other than yourself increases a sense of accomplishment and wellbeing and it just feels good to make someone else happy. What you are doing is fellowship. Fellowship connects you with people with whom you may never have met, had you not had a heart to serve. Having a heart to serve others builds trust. Trust is important as you build a business. Remember Pray, Shift, Move, Serve.

In all this remember God loves you, He is moving you towards walking in your purpose and God will provide new insights along the way. In time as you reach your goals your journey does not stop it just grows and with it the provision of God will grow for you and mentally you will be prepared for all this as you recognize each new season of Prayer/Faith, Prepare, Shift, Serve, and Move.

BY AUTHOR ANGELICA CARMOUCHE

ANGELICA CARMOUCHE

Former United States Navy Corpsman, owner, founder of Angel Market, Kiss My Soap and KMS Home Bath and Body; Angelica Carmouche is an author of five titles to include Faith I Keep, the Little Ethan and Evan children poem book series and a collaborator in Volume One Powerful Affirmations for Fempreneurs headed up by the visionary Nadia Francois. Angelica is a mother of two boys Ethan and Evan Hampton ages

13 and 11 respectfully and is passionate about how positive affirmations and speaking encouragement and

blessings over her life and the lives of her children breathes LIFE into their lives. She has a heart for single moms and believes in encouraging women to be their very best and live their best lives.

Connect with her at: www.angelmarketla.com

He who has a slack hand becomes poor, But the hand of the diligent makes rich.

Proverbs 10:4 NKJV

DAILY AFFIRMATIONS

Today is filled with All the Possibilities

DAY ONE

I have the power to create the life I desire.

DAY TWO

I am strong enough to overcome the challenges in my life.

DAY THREE

I love myself the way that I am.

DAY FOUR

I will do my best to accomplish my goals.

DAY FIVE

I have strengths, abilities and gifts.

DAY SIX

I am enough to be what God wants me to be. I create my own happiness.

DAY SEVEN

My life is filled with abundance, goodness, but most of peace.

BY AUTHOR VANESSA J. ROSS

PRAYER

Dear Lord, as I began my day, I'm asking that you watch over me and please give me the strength and courage to embrace some one else. Lord, help me say mountain get out of my way. Lord, I just say thank you for watching over my family as well as myself. I thank you for keeping me with a sound mind and understanding of your word. Lord, I thank you for healing my body and making me stronger, and peace of mind. Lord, thank you for everything you're doing in my life because, without you I would be nothing. Lord, thank you for loving me for who I am. Therefore Lord, help me to continue to spread the word of your goodness as well as the love, joy and peace all over the world. Lord, I thank you for this day of protection all around me. Lord, I thank you for your grace and mercy. Thank you for just another chance in my life, loving me despite of my sins. Lord, I ask that you continue to bless and keep me throughout each day. In Jesus name I pray. Amen

BY AUTHOR VANESSA J. ROSS

LETTER OF ENCOURAGEMENT

To my dear friend Lynette Elps,

I want you to know that God have you in his hands and no matter what the situation may be, God is in control of the situation. I want you to know that everything is going to work out for your good but, you must have faith in God. Remember that you are strong and you can accomplish anything your heart desires if you only put your trust and believe that God is going to do just what he says he's going to da but, you gotta believe in him totally. Sometimes, we're afraid to step out on faith but, remember God didn't give us a spirit of fear so therefore, this is where your faith must come in. Never let anyone tell you what you can not do because, remember Philippians 4:13 I can do all things through Christ which strengthens me. Now at this point, I need you to put one foot forward and keep it moving.

At this point I want you to remember Jeremiah 29:11 For I know the plans I have for you. I say to you stay focus and remain faithful to the Lord. Don't give up on yourself or feel sorry because, God already knows your situation, and that is not in his plan. You're a survivor and even though you may think there's no way out, we'll think again.

I want you to know and remember that you are *Strong

*Beautiful *Humble *but, most of all, courageous in the sight of God. Lynnette, I want you to know that you are victorious and a powerful woman of God !!!

I leave you with these words, God loves you and so do I and you can't do nothing about it. Always remember that you are a precious gift from God !!!!!

BY AUTHOR VANESSA J. ROSS

VANESSA J. ROSS

I am the second oldest of 9 children, the daughter of Jean Tophia Jack and the late Paul M. Jones Sr. I am a God-fearing woman who loves the Lord with all my heart and soul. I am a mother and a grandmother whose raising my deceased daughter children. I am a member of Believer's Temple of Faith Baptist Church, under the leadership of Pastor Kenneth Davis & First Lady Fay Davis, where I sing in the Chorale Choir, as well as the dance Ministry # Warrior Tribe alongside with Dione Williams. I also sing with Jeffery Pelrean & CTW/ Created To Worship. I am member of Le Bon Ton Baby Doll organization as well as a board member of 108 nonprofit organization in Baltimore MD.

#Author & Co-Author #Motivational/ Inspirational Speaker #Encourager & Songwriter #Owner of #Be Encouraged Christian Apparel #Owner of #I Am Free Active Wear #Author of the Year Award #She Rises Gospel Songwriter's Award

Where there is no vision, the people perish: but he that keepeth the law, happy is he.

Proverbs 29:18 KJV

DAILY AFFIRMATIONS

Soaring to New Heights

DAY ONE

I can do all things through Christ who strengthens me.

DAY TWO

I am the righteousness of God in Christ Jesus.

DAY THREE

My steps are ordered by the Lord daily.

DAY FOUR

I am strong in the Lord and in the power of His might.

DAY FIVE

I am the head and not the tail.

DAY SIX

I am the lender and not the borrower.

DAY SEVEN

I am a chosen generation and a royal priesthood, holy and special.

BY AUTHOR BRENDA SAWYER

PRAYER

Dear Lord Jesus, I pray that You keep Miriam's head lifted unto the hills from where all of her help comes. Let her know that all of her help comes from You. Father continue to order and ordain her steps in the purpose and plan of Your perfect will. Continue to surround Miriam with Your favor as with a shield and dispatch Your angels all around to protect her and keep her safe from all dangers seen and unseen. In Jesus' Name I pray! Amen!

BY AUTHOR BRENDA SAWYER

LETTER OF ENCOURAGEMENT

Dear Miriam,

I am so grateful that God has ordained and connected our paths to meet. You are a blessed Woman of God and certainly a blessing of encouragement to all of the lives that you touch, especially mine. You are the kind of person everyone should have in their circle to propel them to move forward. Your caring, sharing and imparting knowledge reflect your compassion for helping others and keeping them accountably on task. There has never been a time when I came to ask your assistance on a project, that you weren't available for me. Whenever we collaborate on projects together, you always have a word of encouragement that inspires me to keep moving forward. I really admire your business expertise and technology savvy. Speaking of being tech savvy, you have such a talent when it comes to using and creating projects with Canva that has taught me so much. I sometimes call you the "Canva Genius." So whenever I need help with some of the new features on Canva, you can count on me asking you.

You are such a blessing to so many of the clients you coach on a daily basis. You teach and equip them with strategies to believe in themselves and to follow their dreams. Anyone would be honored to have you as their personal coach, because you take the time to work with them and add value to their lives. As you continue to walk out your God-given calling, walk with you head held high, boldly and unapologetically into your destiny.

BY AUTHOR BRENDA SAWYER

BRENDA SAWYER

Brenda Sawyer was born and raised in New York City and currently resides in Philadelphia, PA. She is the Best-Selling Author of Encouraging Words For The Mind, Spirit And Soul, along with other Best-Selling Anthologies and Collaborations. Brenda is the Founder and CEO of GIRLS WALKING WITH INTEGRITY EMPOWERING FOR DESTINY (GWWI)® where she mentors and equips Christian Women with strategies to move from pain to purpose by encouraging, empowering and transforming their lives through Biblical principles and teaching.

Brenda is also the Founder of God Wants To Get The Glory From Your Story©

A series of ongoing one on one Zoom interviews where you can share your testimony in a safe space and give God the Glory for all of His Miracles, Signs and Wonders in your life. When she is not out and about encouraging and transforming the lives of Christian Women, Brenda remains inspired by people and the acquisition of fundamental knowledge. Brenda is also determined to remain a Woman who stays focused on God and to be led by the Holy Spirit. Brenda Sawyer is an exemplary Woman of God, Educator, Exhorter and Servant Leader.

Connect with her at: www.brendasawyer.com

And we know that all things work together for good to those who love God, to those who are the called according to His purpose.

Romans 8:28 NKJV

DAILY AFFIRMATIONS

Consistency

DAY ONE

I am consistent with my prayer life.

DAY TWO

I am consistent in my disciplinary habits.

DAY THREE

Each day I honor my intentions with my actions.

DAY FOUR

I am consistent with my choices and actions.

DAY FIVE

I am consistent in my thinking.

DAY SIX

I am not discouraged by challenges and setbacks.

DAY SEVEN

I create good habits through consistent actions.

BY AUTHOR DR. JOSEPHINE HARRIS

PRAYER

Father, Thank you for the words of your hands because you never stop loving and blessing me. My God, my God, I know that I am weak, and I don't have the power of my own to be consistent in serving you and doing well with others because challenges will come that may want to interrupt my thinking or make me lack consistency, so I ask you Lord to help me to be consistent and overcome any challenges that come my way. Lord, in doing good persistently or in serving you persistently there is always a blessing attached. I want to be blessed Lord, help me to serve you persistently. IN JESUS NAME, AMEN!

BY AUTHOR DR. JOSEPHINE HARRIS

LETTER OF ENCOURAGEMENT

Dear Fellow Woman in Business,

Yes, I am talking to you. Repeat after me, consistency is the key to unlocking doors! First things, I want you to touch yourself on the chest and tell yourself, "I am consistent in my prayer life, my professional life, and my personal life." Second, I want you to believe that you are consistent. You have so many opportunities when you are consistent in your actions and you are more likely to achieve goals, being consistent will make you more productive, more reliable, develop better habits, and generally happier. You don't have to be a perfectionist because you will have some obstacles in your way, but you have the willpower to discipline yourself to achieve your goals and be successful.

Colossians 1:17 states, "And he is before all things, and in him, all things hold together." There is no alternative for consistency when it comes to reaching your goals.

The reason is easy: consistency leads to momentum. The more consistently you do something, the easier it becomes, and the more momentum you build up.

Ultimately, what was once a struggle becomes a habit and habits are difficult to break. But YOU GOT THIS! Because it is the key to making lasting change. So, if you're looking to achieve a goal, REMEMBER to be consistent (no matter what), and ultimately, you'll reach your destination. Now, touch yourself again and repeat after me, "I am consistent in m prayer life, I am consistent in my professional life, and I am consistent in my personal life."

Sincerely,

A Fellow Woman in Business

BY AUTHOR DR. JOSEPHINE HARRIS

DR. JOSEPHINE HARRIS

Modern-day superheroes are not the ones we familiarize with motion pictures, but rather the quintessential professionals; gifted with a sharp sense of servant leadership, willing to show up greatly in the lives of those who need it most. Yielded to this profound ethic; is the multifaceted advocate, Master Coach Dr. Josephine Harris.

Master Coach, Dr. Josephine Harris is a military spouse and Mental Health Expert, a Psychotherapist, a Certified Master Mental Health and Wellness Coach &

Advocate, an International Bestselling author and 9X #1 Times Amazon Bestselling author, Global speaker, philanthropist, serial entrepreneur, Regional Vice President of the HERpernuer Network, and Founder of Calming Minds LLC, a multidimensional coaching practice, helping clients to connect with the mind, body, and soul, by way of inspiration, coaching, and other dynamic mechanisms.

Dr. Harris' mantra is simple: She is inherently committed to emboldening women, particularly military spouses; facilitating for them all, an opportunity of hope.

Connect with her at: www.calmingmindsllc.com

Good planning and hard work lead to prosperity, but hasty shortcuts lead to poverty.

Proverbs 21:5 NLT

DAILY AFFIRMATIONS

Be Ye Transformed to Serve Others

DAY ONE

I am making room in my life for a positive transformation

DAY TWO

My assignment from God will be completed because I am a Blessing to others

DAY THREE

I am committed to serving others

DAY FOUR

I can not go back but moving higher

DAY FIVE

I am on the right path at the right time

DAY SIX

I am heading in the right direction towards my Godly promise

DAY SEVEN

Today I will give focus and attention to those that I've be purposed to serve

BY AUTHOR DR. SANDY SANDERS

PRAYER

Father in Jesus Name I thank you for my dear sister, continue to bless her as she yields to your command according to Ecclesiastes 9:10 Whatsoever thy hand findeth to do, do it with thy might. Help her by guiding her thoughts and hands toward serving others. Thank you that you will hold our hands, and anoint our hands with the power to heal, the power to bring peace, and the power to bring joy in our clients' lives. Thank you that you have chosen us to be your servant in the marketplace and we will be careful to honor you and continue to be thankful for giving us the strategies, gifts, and talents to bless others.

In Jesus' Name Amen

BY AUTHOR DR. SANDY SANDERS

LETTER OF ENCOURAGEMENT

My Dear Sister,

I am so thankful for your courage and boldness to step out on faith and start your business. Truly it has not been "easy" but the most important thing is that you started , you showed up.

Remember that your steps are already ordered by God and that when you show upland determined to help someone be confident that you are solving someone's problem and providing a solution.

Times may be tough and there will be days of uncertainty, however don't take your focus off your mission and God's promise. He has given you the capacity to do what He said you could do. Your business is an assignment from God. Have the faith and continue to network, be flexible and always remember that God is on your side on this journey of entrepreneurship.

Love you in the Lord
Dr. Sandy Sanders, Host and Creator Coffee Conversations With Sandy
A Virtual Talk Show for Authors, Christians Business and Community Leaders

BY AUTHOR DR. SANDY SANDERS

DR. SANDY SANDERS

Dr. Sandy Sanders is, Award-winning Social Media and Podcast Host of Coffee Conversations with Sandy and Friends and Book Talks with Sandy, Dr. Sandy Sanders is an 8x Amazon Best Selling Author, Global Speaker, and Event Moderator.

Dr. Sandy has a great sense of relation with communal advocacy in areas of homelessness, mental health, and reducing recidivism. Dr. Sandy is a licensed Evangelist, recipient of an honorary Humanitarian Doctorate, and active board member of a non-profit organization helping females that are incarcerated.

Loving wife, a devoted mother, and a grandmother of 4.

Connect with her at:

https://www.facebook.com/sandra.sanders3

A Collection of Powerful Prayers for FemPreneurs

PRAYER

Good Morning Prayer

Today is the day the Lord has made. We shall rejoice and be glad in it. Today I pray that all is well with you. Lord I lift up every sister reading this message. Lord right the wrongs in their lives. Strengthen them in their weaknesses. For you are perfect in our time of weakness. Lord take any all things that would try to distract us from you, your word, and your will for our lives. Create in us a clean heart oh God and renew in us a right spirit. And Lord renew our minds. Give us the grace to continue to live out of the newness of mind. Take out anything that's not like you. Today I bind up every sickness and /or disease that would try to overtake any of my sisters and anyone we are connected to. Lord I thank you for this group of mighty women. We will walk in covenant with you and with one another. We will war alongside one another. We unite our faith on behalf of Heavenly Hope Ministries. Thank you for calling us to your powerful ministry. Lord we surrender all to you. Use us as you see fit as we lift and encourage not only one another but our families and church family also. Oh Lord we pray and intercede right now for all those who are hurting in this hour Lord God.

We lift our voices and cry out for those who can't cry out for themselves. Bless us oh God. We praise your holy name. You are worthy Lord God. Speak to our spirit Lord. Reveal that person or persons that needs our prayers right now. Glory to your name. Lord meet every need within this group according to your will. Lord we understand the change we want to see must first begin with us. I surrender. We surrender. Thank you for all you've done. Thank you for all you're doing. Oh Jesus show us your face. Show us you. Show us who you created us to be. Then show how to be. In Jesus name. Amen.

BY AUTHOR DR. FELESHIA YOUNG

PRAYER

Prayer Of Surrender

Father God, in the mighty Name of Jesus, there is no one like You in all the Earth. You are Wonderful, Powerful, Matchless, and Everlasting. Father, you are full of Grace, Mercy and Wisdom. Your Name is above all names. There is none like You. My heart surrenders to You. My hands surrender to You. My gifts and abilities surrender to You. I surrender my plans to You. I surrender my work ethic to You. Father, I surrender my tongue to You. The talents and abilities, that You have given to me, I surrender to You.

Lord, guide my path and teach my hands how to execute. Father, teach me how to finish. Father, grant me the faith and grace to finish the things that You've called me to accomplish. Lord, guide my footsteps so that my feet won't slip. Teach my hands to skillfully execute upon the vision that You have given me. Father, I surrender every area of my life to You. Father, every hidden area I give to You. Lord, I surrender my business, family, career, and ministry to You. Father, I am fully Yours. In Jesus Name. We lift our voices and cry out for those who can't cry out for themselves. Bless us oh God. We praise your holy name. You are worthy Lord God. Speak to our spirit Lord. Reveal that person or persons that needs our prayers right now. Glory to your name. Lord meet every need according to your will. Lord we understand the change we want to see must first begin with us. I surrender. We surrender. Thank you for all you've done. Thank you for all you're doing. Oh Jesus show us your face. Show us you. Show us who you created us to be. Then show how to be. In Jesus name. Amen.

BY AUTHOR DR. FELESHIA YOUNG

PRAYER

Prayer for a Strong Founding Team

Father God in the name of Jesus, God I thank you for blessing me with the vision to birth this business. Father you are faithful to your word and your word will not return to you void. Father I thank you that you will not give me a vision without also giving me provision for the manifestation of what you want to see birthed in the earth. Father I thank you that you have pre-destined individuals to work along side me to build the vision. Now Father I pray that you send them now. I thank you for divine connections. Father you are connecting me to those who have the specific knowledge and resources needed for my business to succeed. Father I thank you for the wisdom to recognize these individuals. In Jesus Name, Amen.

BY AUTHOR DR. FELESHIA YOUNG

PRAYER

Prayer for Skills

Father God I thank you for divine ability and working knowledge. God I thank you for your Holy Spirit living in me leading me and guiding me into all truth. I thank you God for supernatural wisdom to handle the challenges that come with running a business.Father I thank you for Angels on assignment, assigned to me to go before me and make my way straight. Father I thank you that your word says that whatever I put my hands to shall prosper. And Father I give you glory for it! You are God alone!! You are not a man that you should lie. If you said it, it shall come to pass. So Father I thank you for the seed you have planted in me. I will go forth bodly knowing that the entire Kingdom of God is with me and this business you have entrusted me with. I will not doubt myself ever again, because to doubt my ability is to doubt what you have done in me. I repent for anytime I have knowingly or unknowingly believed any lies about me. I am who you say I am God. And I can do what you say I can do!! I am no longer fearful but courageous. In Jesus name. Amen.

BY AUTHOR DR. FELESHIA YOUNG

PRAYER

Prayer for Clients

Heavenly Father God, I am humbled before you. Father I thank you for the grace that is on my life. Father I thank you for trusting me to love as you love. Now Father I thank you that you are sending clients my way. I thank you Lord that this business is ordained by you. Thank you Lord that I never Have to worry or fret about customer and clients to support my business. You have ordained indivduals to seek me out. Father I thank you that those I encounter will not just have an encounter with me but they will encounter you! Father I surrender my will to you. I bind my mind to the mind of Christ and my will to the will of God. You will get glory from each every transaction!! It is not just an earthly transactions but a spiritual one!! Father I will be faithful with the seed. I will sow where you tell me to sow. Father I thank you for exceeding abundant blessing for this business that will run over and touch all that you intend it to bless. In Jesus Name, Amen.

BY AUTHOR DR. FELESHIA YOUNG

PRAYER

Prayer for Goals

Father God in the name of Jesus, Father I thank you for your word which is a lamp unto my feet and a light to my path. Father I thank you that your word says if any man lacks wisdom that he should ask and you will give liberally. So Father I ask that you impart to me Godly wisdom and strategy as I assign goals for the business you have entrusted me with. Father forgive me if I have been thinking too small and limiting your hand. Father you and you alone know the beginning from the end. You knew me before I was in my mother's womb. You have a plan for my life. I plan for good and not evil. You have an expected end for my life and Father I trust you with my whole heart. Now God reveal to me your plan for the next six months, one year, five year and ten year goals. Father I want to be line and in cadence with you. I thank you that you walk with me and I walk with you. I repent for any time I have walked in a spirit of error and poverty. Father I take the limits off. I refuse to be held down or held back by wrong thought processes, stinking thinking, and unforgiveness. Forgive me. Lord I receive your word and apply it to my life and my business. In Jesus name I pray. Amen.

BY AUTHOR DR. FELESHIA YOUNG

DR. FELESHIA BORSKEY YOUNG

Dr. Feleshia Borskey Young is a Licensed Professional Christian Therapist, a Minister, a Motivational Speaker, an Author several books and a visionary. She is the Founder of the 411ForWomen Inc. and the 411ForWomen Foundation. Dr. B Young has accepted her life's assignment to inspire, motivate, and edify others. As a survivor of Domestic Violence and teenage pregnancy, Dr. B Young is passionate about serving the people of God, especially His daughters. Above all her accomplishments Dr. Young considers supporting her husband Apostle Johnny B Young, in ministry and guiding her children

Jairean, Kelsei, Cardarryl and Rushaad to be valuable assets to the Kingdom of God and Society alike, as her primary purpose.

Connect with her at: www.411forwomen.org

> For I know the thoughts that I think toward you, says the Lord, thoughts of peace and not of evil, to give you a future and a hope.
>
> Jeremiah 29:11 NKJV

www.ingramcontent.com/pod-product-compliance
Lightning Source LLC
Chambersburg PA
CBHW070252220526
45465CB00004B/1592